Teaching Elaboration & Word Choice

by LeAnn Nickelsen

SCHOLASTIC
PROFESSIONAL BOOKS

New York • Toronto • London • Auckland • Sydney
Mexico City • New Delhi • Hong Kong • Buenos Aires

I dedicate this book to

Keaton and Aubrey Nickelsen, my twins,
who were nine months old when I finished this book.

Thank you to

* Grapevine-Colleyville School District in Dallas, Texas,
  for all the outstanding staff development it provided.

* Tina Dittrich, friend and teacher, for help with the
  mystery writing lesson.

* Joel, my husband, for his encouragement and for
  helping me find the time to write my books.

* My parents, who continually support and encourage
  me in the education world.

Acknowledgments

Page from *Vocabulary Cartoons* reprinted with permission of the authors: Sam, Max, and Bryan Burchers.
Mystery Story Brainstorming Sheet developed with Tina Dittrich.

Cover design by Sue Kass
Cover illustration by Laura Cornell
Interior illustrations by Teresa Anderko
Interior design by Sydney Wright

ISBN 0-439-09839-4

Contents

Introduction

ALPHABET STEW
Author Unknown

Words can be stuffy, as sticky as glue,
but words can be tutored to tickle you too,
to rumble and tumble and tingle and sing,
to buzz like a bumblebee, coil like a spring.

Juggle their letters and jumble their sounds,
swirl them in circles and stack them in mounds,
twist them and tease them and turn them about,
teach them to dance upside down, inside out.

Make mighty words whisper and tiny words roar
in ways no one ever had thought of before;
cook an improbable alphabet stew,
and words will reveal little secrets to you.

The power of words, chosen carefully and accurately, is fascinating. In order to understand what makes good writing compelling and to help my students develop their writing skills, I reflected on the work of my favorite authors. In doing this, I noticed a common thread: The words these authors chose quickly drew me into the story. These words elicited strong emotions and painted clear, memorable pictures in my imagination—as if I were watching a great movie.

The more words students know, the better able they are to choose words that communicate clearly and explain dynamically. You can help your students develop their word-choice skills in several ways. Have them:

* Read books of many genres with strong description and vocabulary.

* Listen to enriching language.

* Evaluate other writings.

* Learn and practice various ways of elaborating in their own writing.

Jerry Spinelli, one of my favorite authors, has a gift for choosing just the right words and phrases that will spark the reader's curiosity and interest. His book *Maniac Magee* is my favorite and has become my students' favorite fifth-grade novel. *Maniac Magee* opens like this:

> They say Maniac Magee was born in a dump. They say his stomach was a cereal box and his heart a sofa spring. They say he kept an eight-inch cockroach on a leash and that rats stood guard over him while he slept.
>
> *—from* Maniac Magee *by Jerry Spinelli.*
> *Copyright 1991 by Jerry Spinelli.*
> *Published by HarperCollins.*

After we read the book, I asked my students why they enjoyed it so much. I got a variety of answers, but number one was: The author used specific, precise words that make the characters and plot come alive and that we kids can relate to. These words also sparked curiosity. The students wondered why Maniac Magee had a pet cockroach eight inches long, and who is this Maniac anyway who would want this kind of a pet?

Providing students with good literature that incorporates varied and colorful word choice is a great way to help them elaborate on their own writing. Kids need examples that they can emulate. In this book I provide examples of novels and short picture books that you can read to students to give them a good sense of how elaboration through good word choice can enhance their own writing. And I include activities to help students choose dynamic words that will make their writing come alive as they practice the writing process.

Chapter 1

Elaboration and Word-Choice Lessons

Elaboration is an important key to making writing come alive. Introduce your students to this concept by telling them that by choosing the right words to use in their writing (word choice) and adding the right words (elaboration) they can communicate their ideas better and make their stories and reports more exciting. Explain that they can build the vocabulary they use every day in speaking and writing by reading books, learning new words, and listening to people speak. Let them know that each vocabulary word that they learn is an accomplishment and will make a difference to their writing.

Elaboration and Word Choice Are . . .

* using specific and accurate words that create the desired meaning
* using lively verbs, colorful adjectives, and specific nouns
* incorporating striking words and phrases that readers won't forget
* selecting words that linger in the reader's mind and create curiosity
* choosing natural and individualistic words that portray the author's personality
* adding specific and precise details (words and phrases) to descriptions

How to Create Language Lessons That Build Elaboration and Word-Choice Skills

A good way to begin building elaboration and word-choice skills is to link these concepts to your language arts lessons. For example, once students know what a verb is, they can learn how to choose better verbs to make their writing more exciting. They

also can learn how to find verbs in other people's writing and evaluate whether a better verb could have been chosen for a particular sentence. What follows is an example of how I create an elaboration and word-choice skill lesson on action verbs. This will serve as a model for other lessons I suggest, beginning on page 9.

✳ A Sample Lesson: Action Verbs

Beginning each lesson with a motivator (anticipatory set) will heighten student interest. I often use picture books, a section of a novel, stories, or quotes that help students focus on the concept I'm introducing. For example, to build word-choice and elaboration skills during a lesson on verbs, I might read a few pages from *Maniac Magee*. The author's wonderful verb choices are always a hit with kids and help open their eyes to all kinds of action-verb possibilities.

At the start of each lesson, I also give students their own copies of the Elaboration Skill Web (page 15). They label it according to the skill being studied and fill it in as we work together.

Next we follow the seven steps on the web sheet. These may vary a bit according to the concept you're studying.

Step 1. Define the concept and have students, as a class, write the definition or list of characteristics on the web sheet beside number 1. For example, provide and discuss a definition such as the following for action verbs:

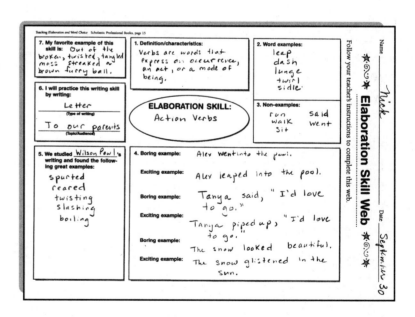

Action verbs are words that express an act, occurrence, or mode of being. In his book *On Writing Well*, William Zinsser said, "Verbs are the most important of all your tools. They push the sentence forward and give it momentum . . . *flail, poke, dazzle, squash, beguile, pamper, swagger, wheedle, vex.*"

Now fill in the characteristics with the class.

Step 2. As a class, have students generate a list of words or an example of the skill topic.

Step 3. As a class, have students generate a list of (or just one) non-examples.

Step 4. Give students one boring example; then ask them to brainstorm ways of making the example exciting. Fill in the first example as a class. Then have the students work in pairs to create the next two boring and exciting examples. Share the students' examples and discuss other possibilities. Stress that there's no one right way.

Step 5. Study someone else's good example of this writing skill. Photocopy a page or paragraph from a book or magazine onto a transparency and put it on the overhead so everyone can see it. I've also used the best of student writing from past years or some of my own writing to illustrate the particular concept. (Students love to see what their teacher wrote.) In any case, highlight the examples and have students write these on their sheets. Besides *Maniac Magee* by Jerry Spinelli, books I've used successfully for the action-verb lesson include: *Brave Irene* by William Steig and *I Think I Thought* by Marvin Terban.

Step 6. Now it's time for you to decide on a writing assignment for the students to use to practice this skill or concept. Students will use more than one skill—maybe many skills—for the assignment, but you should evaluate only the taught skill. This will help students focus on exactly what that skill looks like in their writing. For example, you may want the whole class to practice writing a friendly letter. Or you may want to let students choose from several appropriate types of writing. I usually have the students do the same type of writing at first. Once they are used to the process, I may give them a choice.

Provide students with a copy of the Brainstorm Sheet (page 16) and the Writing Organization Sheet (page 17). Model how to complete the Brainstorm Sheet. Show them how to develop a rubric. (See Chapter 4 for more information on evaluation.) Remind students that you will grade their writing according to the

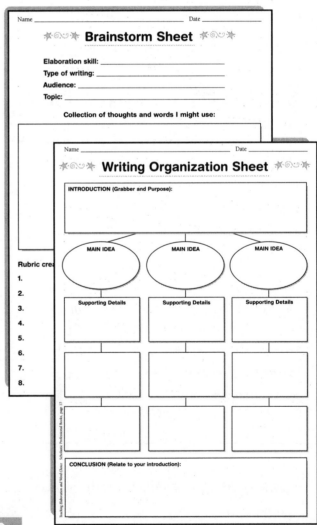

```
                                    456 Wixon Road
                                    West Chester, OH 45040
                                    September 4, 2000

Dear Mom and Dad,

        I know you won't believe what I am about to tell you, so I thought I
would write you a letter so you would at least read what happened rather than
hear me tell you this extraordinary event.
        It was a normal day of recess. The sun was shining brightly. The
students were laughing, yelling and screaming. I, of course, was the coolest
kid out on the soccer field while other boys dashed back and forth on the
basketball court. The teacher, Mrs. Yikes, was marching back and forth in
her section of the field encouraging students to slide down the slide properly.
        Out of nowhere, a huge, thunderous bang shook the earth. All of the
students gasped and looked up into the sky to find to our amazement, a
cumulous, thundercloud as large as the Star Trek spacecraft. It hovered over
all of us spitting out rain. This rain started to fall like golf-ball size hail on
our skin. In a split second, students began screaming and stampeding back
and forth to avoid the hard rain.
        While I was running, I tripped and fell into a huge pit which led me to
this dark, eerie cave. It was like a dungeon you would see in a castle story.
It was as dark as Darth Vador's cape with the sounds of bats beating their
wings and echoes of water dripping onto the hard, pointy rocks. Fear
overwhelmed me. I tried to yell, but it only echoed back at me and scared me
worse. Then, I heard the recess whistle.
        Whew! I stopped daydreaming to find myself against the school wall.
You see, I really did have an awful recess because I was confined to the wall
because I pulled Suzy Smith's hair. At least, while I was against the prison, I
envisioned this very creative, imaginative, story. Aren't you proud of me?

                                    Sincerely,

                                    Brad Ott
```

rubric you create together using the Brainstorm Sheet. Also make it clear that they will be responsible for developing their own rubrics on future pieces of writing.

Step 7. Have students choose their favorite example of the elaboration skill. Examples may come from a book, you, or another student, or they can be a collaborative class effort. This step helps students construct their own understanding using newly learned information.

Starters for More Lessons

Here are definitions, examples, and good books to get you started on elaboration and word-choice lessons for the other language concepts—adjectives and adverbs, description and detail, dialogue, setting, similes, superlatives, comparisons and analogies, rhyme, examples and personal anecdotes, metaphors, personification, quotations, and synonyms. These are just suggestions. There are many other jumping-off points.

Adjectives and Adverbs

Definition: *An adjective is a word that describes a noun.*
What better way to add color and detail to nouns than with adjectives?
Boring example: She wore a gown and long gloves.
Elaborated example: Her silky, jeweled gloves extended to the large, puffed sleeves of her elegant gown.

Definition: *An adverb describes a verb, usually by answering the questions How, When, or Where. Adverbs often end in* ly.
Boring example: She slept on the bed.
Elaborated example: She slept violently, tossing and turning during her horrendous nightmare.

Good books to use:
* *Charlie and the Chocolate Factory* by Roald Dahl
* *The View From Saturday* by E. L. Konigsburg
* *Animalia* by Graeme Base
* *Maxie* by Mildred Kantrowitz
* *The Z was Zapped* by Chris Van Allsburg
* *Many Luscious Lollipops* by Ruth Heller

Description and Detail

Definition: *Description is communication intended to give a mental picture of something. Including specific details can help to do this.*
In addition to adjectives and adverbs, prepositional phrases can add more detail. They make it easier for the reader to visualize or relate a subject to something he or she already knows.
Boring example: He was wearing shoes.
Elaborated example: He wore perfect-fitting cowboy boots with stitched cactus designs on the sides and spurs on each high, square heel.

Good books to use:
* *Shrek!* by William Steig
* *Rosie's Walk* by Pat Hutchins
* *21 Balloons* by William Pene du Bois
* *Where the Red Fern Grows* by Wilson Rawls
* *The House of Dies Drear* by Virginia Hamilton
* *The Giver* by Lois Lowry

> **TEACHER TIP**
> For such skills as Description and Detail, Dialogue, and Examples and Personal Anecdotes, you'll probably have room for only one example on the Elaboration Skill Web.

Dialogue

Definition: *Dialogue is the talking between characters in a story. (Internal dialogue is when characters talk or think to themselves.)*
Conversation is a great way to elaborate on a person's feelings or tone while keeping the story line flowing. The use of conversation embellishes the writer's thoughts. It can also help the reader feel the emotion through the character's point of view.
Boring example: The bird was brave.
Elaborated example: And then the little bird said in a soft, calm voice, "Do not be afraid of this creature; he is a friend to everyone."

Good books to use:

* *Maniac Magee* by Jerry Spinelli
* *The Best School Year Ever* by Barbara Robinson
* *The Stinky Cheese Man and Other Fairly Stupid Tales* by Jon Scieszka and Lane Smith
* *The Phantom Tollbooth* by Norman Juster

Setting

Definition: *Setting is the time and place of a story.*
Details about setting are especially significant in descriptive writing. They help the reader accurately visualize the scene—actually "walk" through the setting.
Boring example: He was sitting near the table.
Elaborated example: A striped cloth covered the kitchen table he was sitting near.

Good books to use:

* *The Lion, the Witch and the Wardrobe* by C. S. Lewis
* *Summer of the Monkey* by Wilson Rawls
* *In the Attic* by Haiwyn Oram
* *The Salamander Room* by Anne Mazer

Similes

Definition: *Similes are figures of speech comparing two unlike things. They are introduced by* like, as, *or* as if.
Comparisons using similes creatively clarify a writer's thoughts and give the reader an insight into the writer's world.
Examples: In some ways, an old friend is like a comfortable old shoe. The runner was as fast as the wind.

Good books to use:

* *Maniac Magee* by Jerry Spinelli
* *Hailstones and Halibut Bones* by Mary O'Neil
* *Owl Moon* by Jane Yolen
* *Storm in the Night* by Mary Stolz
* *Borrowed Black* by Ellen Bryan Obed
* *Quick as a Cricket* by Audrey Wood
* *The Elephant's Child* by Rudyard Kipling

Superlatives

Definition: *A superlative form of an adjective compares three or more things.*
Superlatives can make statements more meaningful, emphatic, and often exaggerated.
Boring examples: Yesterday was an exasperating day! The diamond is bright.
Elaborated examples: Yesterday was the most exasperating day I have ever had in my life! This is the brightest diamond I've ever seen.

Good books to use:
* *Little Women* by Louisa May Alcott
* Any piece of literature will include superlatives.

Comparisons and Analogies

Definition: *Comparisons and analogies compare two or more items to establish similarities and differences as well as provide perspective.*
Using comparisons and analogies is a great way to explain abstract concepts. If the writer can compare an abstract concept to something concrete or something most readers are familiar with, it's more likely to be understood.
Elaborated examples: If you wanted to count from one to one million, it would take you about twenty-three days. The whale shark is as big as a school bus.

Good books to use:
* *What's Smaller Than a Pygmy Shrew?* by Robert E. Wells
* *Is a Blue Whale the Biggest Thing There Is?* by Robert E. Wells
* *How Much Is a Million?* by David M. Schwartz
* *James and the Giant Peach* by Roald Dahl
* *Yellow & Pink* by William Steig

Rhyme

Definition: *Rhymes are words that end with the same sound (hot and pot, Billy and silly). Some poetry lines end with rhyming words.*
Because our brain picks up on patterns and similarities, using rhymes is fun and intriguing. Poetry is full of rhyming words.
Examples: He who drives a safer way will live to drive another day.
The corn is as high as an elephant's eye.

Good books to use:
* *Antics* by Cathi Hepworth
* All of Shel Silverstein's books

❋ *The Scholastic Rhyming Dictionary* (This is a MUST!)

Examples and Personal Anecdotes

Definitions: *Examples are specific descriptions, stories, or words that clarify a larger theme being presented. One very effective kind of example is the personal anecdote. An anecdote is a brief story used to make a point.*

A writer can clarify his or her thoughts by including examples. Personal stories are a great way to catch the reader's attention because everyone is interested in what other people do and think. Examples make things more understandable by relating something unknown to something familiar.

Example: When I was eight years old, I learned firsthand why it's important to know what to do if there's a fire. When fire broke out in our house, I had to escape from my flaming room by using the ladder kept outside my bedroom window. Knowing what to do saved my life. Have a plan ready!

TEACHER TIP
You won't need to use the Elaboration Skill Web for Examples and Personal Anecdotes. After providing students with the definition and examples, write an anecdote with the class. Then have each student write his or her own personal anecdote.

Good books to use:

❋ Autobiographies and memoirs
❋ Teachers, it's time for you to write! Students love to hear your personal anecdotes.

Metaphors

Definition: *Metaphors are figures of speech in which a word or phrase literally denoting one kind of object or idea is used in place of another to suggest a likeness. The comparisons are made without using the word* like *or* as.

Metaphors add vividness to writing. They can help an abstract idea become more real and connected to what a reader already knows.

Boring examples: I was mad! The wind blew across the driveway on that windy morning.

Elaborated examples: My cheeks were flaming with anger. The leaf tripped across the driveway on that windy morning.

Good books to use:
❋ *Say Something* by Mary Stoltz
❋ *Miracle Tree* by Christobel Mattingley
❋ *The Patchwork Cat* by William Mayne
❋ *Once I Was Scared* by Helena Pittman

Personification

Definition: *Personification is a figure of speech in which an idea, object, or animal is given qualities of a person.*

Personification makes writing more interesting and creative. It is especially useful for bringing poetry to life.

Boring example: The trees were rustling.

Elaborated example: The trees seemed to whisper among themselves as if they wondered what would happen next.

Good books to use:

* *The People Could Fly* by Virginia Hamilton
* *My Secret Surprise* by Jasper Tomkins
* *Winter Barn* by Peter Parnell

Quotations

Definition: *A quotation is an excerpt from a speech or passage. A quote is usually included in a piece of writing because it is particularly thought-provoking.*

Quotes can extend or clarify a writer's thoughts and encourage the reader to meditate on the deeper meanings of the text.

Example: "Play hard, but play fair," said my dad as I headed out to the hockey rink.

Good books to use:

* *Ben and Me* by Robert Lawson
* *Number the Stars* by Lois Lowry
* Autobiographies/biographies

Synonyms

Definition: *Synonyms are words that have similar meanings.*

When writers know many words that mean the same thing, they have a larger word bank to choose from when they are stuck on just how to write what they're thinking. Teach students how to use the thesaurus to find fresh words.

Boring example: Ebony looked happy at her party.

Elaborated example: Ebony looked radiant at her party.

Good books to use:

* *Abel's Island* by William Steig
* *Walking Is Wild, Weird, and Wacky* by Karen Kerber
* Thesaurus (A must!)

Name _____ Date _____

✦✦✦ **Elaboration Skill Web** ✦✦✦

Follow your teacher's instructions to complete this web.

2. Word examples:

3. Non-examples:

1. Definition/characteristics:

ELABORATION SKILL:

4. Boring example:

Exciting example:

Boring example:

Exciting example:

Boring example:

Exciting example:

7. My favorite example of this skill is:

6. I will practice this writing skill by writing:

_____
(Type of writing)

_____
(Topic/Audience)

5. We studied _____'s writing and found the following great examples:

✴⚘✴ Brainstorm Sheet ✴⚘✴

Elaboration skill: _____

Type of writing: _____

Audience: _____

Topic: _____

Collection of thoughts and words I might use:

Rubric creation:

1.

2.

3.

4.

5.

6.

7.

8.

Name _____ Date _____

 # Writing Organization Sheet

INTRODUCTION (Grabber and Purpose):

MAIN IDEA

MAIN IDEA

MAIN IDEA

Supporting Details

Supporting Details

Supporting Details

CONCLUSION (Relate to your introduction):

Chapter 2

Elaboration and Word Choice During the Writing Process

Word choice can make a piece of writing come alive or fall flat, be memorable or forgettable. It's extremely important in every written piece. If you teach and discuss word choice before students begin their assignments, you'll see a difference in the results.

Marjorie Frank, author of *If You're Trying to Teach Kids How to Write, You've Gotta Have This Book!*, proposes a nine-step writing plan that emphasizes the importance of word choice. Below I outline an adaptation of her plan that works well with my writing lessons. You probably won't want to go through all nine steps with every piece of writing. Instead, you can choose which steps are needed for each assignment.

A Nine-Step Plan Integrating Word Choice

Step 1. Motivation

Do something that will grab students' attention and entice them to get excited about the topic or genre you're studying.

* Read a book together.
* Walk students through an intriguing experience.
* Ask a question that kindles their curiosities.
* Introduce an interesting newspaper or magazine story.
* Set up a scenario and ask them what will happen next.

* Show them an example of your own writing.
* Discuss a movie story line.
* Show an object(s) pertaining to the writing topic

I frequently present the short story "Judy and the Volcano" by Wayne Harris. The story features Judy, a student who can't write a decent story. During a detention period she comes up with such a good one that she's asked to read it at a schoolwide assembly. The story helps students realize that writing can be frustrating and takes time and imagination, but it gives you a great feeling of success when it's completed, shared, and published.

Step 2. Word Catching

Next comes the word-catch session—brainstorming words, phrases, and ideas that can be used for this particular piece of writing. This step, which is the most neglected in the writing process yet most important for improving word choice, encourages focused thinking and elaboration. As you assign writing projects and study various topics throughout the year, have students brainstorm for unique and useful words and phrases related to those topics. For example, some of the topics I've brainstormed with my students are mystery words, nature words, ocean words, funny words, and serious words. I encourage students to jot down any interesting words or phrases they come across during the year on a sheet of paper (one sheet per word category) and store these sheets in a "Word-Catch Categories" section of their writing notebooks. (See Chapter 5 for a detailed description of writing notebooks.)

Word-Catch Category—Mystery Words and Phrases

eerie	foul smell
door creaking	suspense
howling wind	heart beating rapidly
whirling wind	tiptoe through the hall
dark	lonely
fearful	full moon
shadowy clouds	

Word-Catch Categories

Here are just some of the categories your students may want to develop word lists for. The whole class can brainstorm words to fit a chosen category as it comes up in the classroom. All students can add the page to the word-catch section of their writing notebooks (see Chapter 5). They can refer to this resource throughout the year to have a ready supply of interesting words for their writing.

Suggested Categories

color	time	friendly	unfriendly
city	country	day	night
foreign	home	school	theater
food	ocean	valley	hill
jungle	mountain	desert	seashore
shopping	appreciation	disappointment	clothing
suspense	fat	thin	dinosaur
computer	holiday	cartoon	hate
adventure	store	family	love
hate	hot	cold	circus
hello	airplane	train	automobile
swimming	football	gold	space
advertising	tennis	baseball	basketball
scratchy	yes	no	sleep
song	drink	election	size
shape	war	peace	season
weather	radio	TV	career
baby	children	teenage	adult
teacher	fear	music	mineral
plant	animal	restaurant	health

As students start collecting and sharing favorite words, they soon begin using this new vocabulary in their speaking and writing. I frequently set aside class time for students to share their word catches. And during the year, as I teach various concepts such as idioms, personification, famous quotes, and writing personal anecdotes, we have word-catch brainstorming sessions based on these. A sample idioms list is included below.

Word-Catching Category—Idioms

Don't make a mountain out of a molehill.	You really have a green thumb.
It's time to hit the road.	That sounds like it's up my alley.
I've got it right on the tip of my tongue.	I wish he'd go fly a kite.
You hit the nail on the head.	I think we'd better throw in the towel.
It's been raining cats and dogs all day.	I'm afraid we bought a lemon.
I've got butterflies in my stomach.	She's pulling your leg.
He's as sharp as a tack.	There he goes crying wolf again.
I think he's got something up his sleeve.	That's like the pot calling the kettle black.
I'm all thumbs.	We'd better keep tabs on him.

Creating these word-catch resources provides students with their own personal word and phrase lists to help them build strong word choice within every piece of writing.

Step 3. Organization

After students have brainstormed for words and phrases, they should think about how to organize their writing. Give students the following hints for organizing their ideas.

* Create a graphic organizer or outline for the particular type of writing. (Students can also use the organizer on page 17.)
* Sequence the ideas (introduction, paragraph 1, paragraph 2, paragraph 3, conclusion).
* Include words and phrases you like in the graphic organizer so you'll use them.
* Feel free to change your plan during rough-draft writing. It's just a plan.

Step 4. Rough Draft

Now that students have their thoughts, feelings, phrases, words, and organizational plan, they're ready to write their first draft. Have them write without stopping to correct spelling or punctuation or to think of the best way to express an idea. Encourage them to talk about their ideas with their classmates during this step. Explain that this is a very rough draft and that they'll have a chance to refine "sloppy copy" later.

Step 5. Rereading for Sense and Readability

At this point students have a chance to proofread their writing. Does it make sense? Do I like the story flow? Could I add more action? One of the best ways for students to find awkward words, phrases, and sentences is to read their piece aloud (to themselves). I usually provide a Word-Choice Checklist (page 54) for them to refer to. Students understand that the checklist will also be used when their writing is evaluated.

Step 6. Sharing for Response

Now students trade papers with a partner to get feedback. I make the listeners responsible for writing down three things they liked about their partner's work and two areas where the student can improve and grow. Tell students that this is not the time to look at the mechanics of the paper; it's an opportunity to give feedback on ideas and word choice.

Step 7. Editing and Mechanics Check

Now is the time for students to fill out a rubric such as A Complete Writing Checklist (pages 57–58) or another rubric you have created for the specific writing assignment. Editing is done right on the rough draft. With another student or two (the more the better), students check off the rubric evaluation sheet to make sure that the writing focused on the elements outlined in the assignment or rubric, and they make any necessary changes on their rough copies. Then, taking into consideration the advice of their partner or group, the students also mark corrections of their spelling, punctuation, capitalization, and so on. The teacher then takes these sloppy copies filled with editing marks and reviews them for more mechanical errors and word-choice ideas. (You may want to mark your suggestions with a different color pencil.) You can do this in whatever way works for you—by reading the papers independently, conferencing with the child, reading over his or her shoulder, or asking parents or a teacher aide to help.

Step 8. The Final Copy

Have students use the marked-up copy to write a final copy taking all the suggestions into consideration. Remind them one more time to be sure to get rid of those taboo

words (words used too frequently) and to replace them with some challenging words from the word-catch section of their writing notebook.

✸ Step 9. The Presentation

Finally it's time to show off! Help students be creative in displaying their works of art (see Scholastic's *Books Don't Have to Be Flat* by Kathy Pike and Jean Mumper). There are so many ways to display and present writing. For example, students can staple their story onto a construction-paper likeness of their main character, decorate a cereal box, create a poster, or design a mini book jacket. After the displays are completed, have a read-aloud session. Encourage students to read with expression and enthusiasm to capture the audience's attention. This is a great time for you to evaluate. As you listen carefully to the story, check off the rubric. I always go back through the stories to check the mechanics of the paper, but I save a lot of time by evaluating the content of the writing during the read-aloud.

The following writing process lesson focuses on mystery and suspense writing, but you can adapt it and the worksheets that follow it to other forms of writing.

A Mystery Writing Lesson

An example of a lesson using the Nine-Step Writing Process Plan
Time line: 3–5 days

Objectives

✸ Students will brainstorm to create a list of suspenseful words or phrases and add them to the word-catch section of their writing notebooks.

✸ Students will use these words or phrases appropriately in their writing in order to improve their word choice and to create a suspenseful mystery story.

✸ Students will use the Nine-Step Writing Process Plan to complete a story that includes most of the characteristics of a mystery.

Motivation

1. With the lights dimmed, read the short suspense story, "A Realtor's Reality," at the end of this chapter. Put it on an overhead so students can see and hear the words at the same time.

2. Discuss what made the story so suspenseful. Which phrases and words do students remember the most vividly?

3. Discuss and teach students the components of a mystery story. (See Characteristics of a Mystery Story on page 27. You might make copies for each student or use it on the overhead.)

Procedure

1. Have students work in small groups to create their own suspenseful word and phrase list. Next have the groups share their words and phrases as a whole class. Write them on the board so students can write them correctly on their word-catch lists. We brainstormed for words in two categories: suspenseful verbs and suspenseful nouns/phrases. Following are just a few of the words we came up with:

Suspenseful Verbs	*Suspenseful Nouns/Phrases*
shattered	silent whispers
CREEAAK	croaking frog
startled	tiptoe walking
screamed	thunderous storm
lurking	electrifying lightning

> **TEACHER TIP**
>
> The story on pages 25–26 is great for motivating students to elaborate and make interesting word choices. To help students better understand the mystery story genre, you may want to read aloud or have them read mystery stories such as "The Adventure of the Speckled Band" by Arthur Conan Doyle.

2. Invite students to use their prior knowledge to practice elaborating on sample sentences. Use the examples here to model how to elaborate on a simple sentence.
Original: The boy went home.
Revised: The frightened boy walked down the dark, lonely street toward home.

Original: The house looked haunted.
Revised: The wind was howling and the trees were creaking. The old, weather-beaten house looked haunted.

3. Set up a brainstorming session (see Mystery Story Brainstorming Sheet, page 28) to identify the specific mystery story elements students plan to use in their story. Make sure students use words from their word-catch lists. Also provide students with a copy of the Mystery Story Rubric (page 29) so they understand how they will be evaluated.

4. Have students organize their words and ideas using the graphic organizer (like the one on page 17) or an outline to sequence the elements of their writing, then write their rough drafts.

5. After the students write their rough drafts, have them read them aloud to themselves. This is the best way to identify awkward words, sentence fragments, and other common mistakes. It also gives them the chance to be the first to evaluate their work.

6. Now it's time for peer editing. Partner the students and give each a Peer Editing Sheet (page 30). As you can see, this sheet is tailored to the mystery writing genre. You can adapt this to fit your particular genre or assignment. First, students read the entire story silently. Next, they read it to fill out the sheet. Finally, the partners explain to each other why they wrote what they did on the editing sheet.

7. Partner students again (same or different partners) and have them check each other.

8. Have students use their evaluation sheets (self- and peer-editing sheets), rough drafts, and word-catch lists to write their final copies.

9. Encourage students to present their work creatively. I have my students use construction paper and crayons or markers to make super-sleuth cutouts to which they attach their final copies. Last, have students read their final copies aloud to the class while you use the point system on the Mystery Story Rubric (page 29). (Of course you can adapt this sheet to fit other types of writing.)

Read the following mystery story for Writing Process Step 1: Motivation.

A Realtor's Reality

Shortly after I received my real estate license and was in the process of opening my own office, a phone call came in. To my surprise, I was offered my first listing. The call was unusual, though, because the two-story, English Tudor-style house the caller wanted to list had been vacant for many years, and it was known in the real estate trade as a lemon. In fact, it was nicknamed the Second Addams Family House. Nevertheless, needing the business, I agreed to go and appraise the house.

First I told several of my friends about what I was doing, and one of my closest friends, who was extremely curious, asked if he could accompany me. We agreed to meet at the house the following Saturday at 6:00 P.M.

On the way over to the house, the sky darkened with thick, purple-gray thunderclouds. Not knowing if the house had electricity, I took a flashlight. As I stood in the yard waiting for my friend, it became extremely dark and started to pour. I had to go in without him. As I headed for the rickety front porch, I could see why the house was referred to as a lemon. It was badly weather-beaten, the paint had peeled, the shingles were falling off, and the shrubbery was terribly overgrown.

When I opened the heavy, thick door, I was greeted by an enormous cobweb, which stuck to my face like glue. While fumbling around for the lights, I thought to myself that a lot of work was needed before this house would be marketable. After turning on the lights and getting only a glimpse of the inside, there was a brilliant streak of lightning followed by a sudden clap of thunder.

The lights went out.

I switched on my flashlight. The beam of light stopped first on a broken-down chair draped in a dusty, moth-eaten gray blanket. As I moved the light slowly around the room, I spotted what appeared to be someone's coat bunched up in the corner, and on the floor in the middle of the room was a lone candle stub.

Just then I became aware of the sounds around me. There was a scratching and scraping to my right, a soft scurrying coming through the archway that led to the next room, and overhead there seemed to be a beckoning whisper that started to draw me in the direction of the old circular staircase. I was sure it was my imagination, but as I got closer to the stairs the soft whispering seemed to be calling my name: M...m...a...a...r..r..y...y...

I started up the stairs, feeling the need to check out the second floor before I finished looking over the first floor. Again I heard the whispering, and now it seemed louder: M...m...a...a...r..r..y...y... My mind told me this wasn't possible—it was only my nerves. However, my stomach had begun to tighten, and the palms of my hands were sweaty. With my heart racing, I continued up the stairs with only my flashlight to show me the way, uncertain of what lay ahead.

By this time the sky was pitch black, the thunder was rolling, the wind was howling, and the shutters were banging against the house. Mother Nature's per-cussion was disturbing. The stairs creaked loudly, and they seemed unsteady with each upward step. Suddenly, something brushed against my foot, but when I shone the light down, nothing was there. Then something seemed to rush by my head—again nothing. By the time I reached the top, I wasn't so sure I could go on. Barely a whisper above the storm, I heard it again: M...m...a...a...r..r..y...y... I summoned up all of the courage I had left and turned down the hallway. I know it sounds crazy, but I was not about to be called the Wimpy Realtor.

Several doors lined the hallway. The whispering had to be coming from one of them. With a swift movement I swung open one of the doors. Nothing was in the room except cobwebs. I moved down the hall and cautiously opened the next door. Before I could shine my light around that room, the lightning streaked and there was a loud crash. I quickly closed the door and decided that it wasn't that important to find out if the sound came from that room.

By now I'd had enough and decided the sale wasn't worth all of this. As I turned around to leave, I again heard the whispering. I couldn't let it go. I had to check it out. With my heart pulsating, I slowly crept to the final door. Before I could turn the knob ... the door slowly swung open....I heard loud, hysterical laughter and many voices shouting, "HAPPY BIRTHDAY, MARY!"

Characteristics of a Mystery Story

1. A baffled friend or observer usually tells the story and becomes a sleuth.

2. A crime is committed against a person (robbery, blackmail, murder), a place (vandalism), or an object (theft). The crime must be important enough for the sleuth and reader to try to solve it.

3. The crime is discovered.

4. The sleuth checks to see if there are any witnesses, fingerprints, and evidence. He or she also determines what is known and what has been seen or heard.

5. The relevancy of each clue is decided. Sometimes there are red herrings to temporarily throw off a sleuth.

6. Suspects and motives are considered. The suspects must have motives, but these are not always obvious. The sleuth may have to delve deeply into the suspect's past.

7. A chase may occur.

8. At some point the sleuth reveals the solution with step-by-step explanations of the detection and deductions that led to the solution. (The clues the sleuth used must have been made available to the reader as well.)

9. Justice always prevails, even though it may not be given in a court.

Name _____ Date _____

✦ Mystery Story ✦
Brainstorming Sheet

Use the following questions to plan your mystery story. Also remember to include some of your word-catch words as you brainstorm.

1. Who is telling the story? Who are some of the characters? (Describe their personalities.)

2. What is (are) the setting(s)? Describe it (them).

3. What crime is committed? In other words, what is your story's problem?

4. How was the crime discovered? Who discovered it? What is the solution?

5. How and when will you introduce the sleuth?

6. Who were the witnesses? What clues did they provide? What did they see, hear, smell, taste?

7. What are at least three clues that will help solve the mystery? Who will discover them?

8. Who are your suspects and what were their motives?

9. Is there going to be a chase? Who? Where? Why?

10. Who is the villain? What was his or her motive? Include a step-by-step explanation of how the case was solved. This will go at the end of your story.

Before reading the resolution of your story aloud to the class, have your classmates try to solve the mystery. Make sure that they have enough information to make a good guess and that your story is logical—the times and events must coordinate.

Name _____ Date _____

 # Mystery Story Rubric

Author: _____

Evaluating teacher: _____

CRITERIA	Not Yet	OK	WOW!
1. Brainstorm sheet is attached and completed.	I	2	3
2. Includes a strong introduction (quote, story fact, startling phrase, question).	I	2	3
3. Has an effective conclusion (wrapped up the mystery; related back to introduction).	I	2	3
4. Variety of words are used; taboo words are avoided.	I	2	3
5. Includes lively verbs and lots of adjectives.	I	2	3
6. Suspenseful phrases and words are included.	I	2	3
7. Has most of the mystery characteristics.	I	2	3
8. Grammar, spelling, and punctuation are correct.	I	2	3
9. Read with expression.	I	2	3
10. Presentation was interesting and neatly done.	I	2	3

Total possible points: 30   **Total points:** _____

I like the following about your mystery:

_____

_____

_____

_____

Here's one way to improve this mystery:

_____

_____

_____

_____

✦❀✧❀❀ Peer Editing Sheet ❀❀✧❀✦

Mystery Story Title: _____

The mystery story is written by: _____

The peer editor is: _____

1. You have included the following mystery characteristics:

_____

_____

2. I saw the following lively, active verbs (not boring ones like *said*):

_____

3. You used the following interesting nouns, adjectives, and adverbs
(not taboo words like nice, fun, scared):

_____

_____

4. You used the following similes and metaphors to create suspense:

_____

_____

5. I thought that the following suspenseful words and phrases were
especially effective:

_____

_____

6. Three things I liked most about your story are:

_____

_____

_____

7. Two suggestions I have for your story are:

_____

_____

8. Your story has:
- ✳ a strong introduction
- ✳ an effective conclusion
- ✳ dialogue between characters

Chapter 3

Elaboration and Word-Choice Activities

Here are some of my favorite elaboration and word-choice activities. They are great ways for you to reinforce the skills lessons presented in Chapter 1. You can tailor them for your grade level and your students' special needs.

Interactive Bulletin Boards

There are lots of possibilities for creating interactive synonym bulletin boards that will help students to avoid taboo words and build their vocabularies. I include suggestions for two bulletin boards that my students have enjoyed.

✦ Blooming Words

On flower-with-stem cutouts (page 40), have students display the vague, overused, boring word in the center and the synonyms on the flower petals. One flower per word will brighten the classroom.

✦ Synonym Scoop Ice Cream Parlor

On cone cutouts (page 41), have students display a vague, overused, or boring word. Varied, unique synonym words should be written on scoops of ice cream. Be colorful with the scoops since it's those unique, varied words that add color to a piece of writing. Have several cones around the classroom and call it the Synonym Scoop Ice Cream Parlor.

Graphic Organizers

Graphic organizers provide your visual learners with a way to easily remember information.

✦ Synonym Circles

I have my students list their taboo words in their writing notebooks (see Chapter 5 for a detailed description of writing notebooks) on a synonym circle worksheet (page 42). Students can refer to the taboo words every time they write since they keep these notebooks on their desks during writing time.

✦ Webbing

For variety, you may want to use the web template (page 42). The synonyms radiate from the center taboo word.

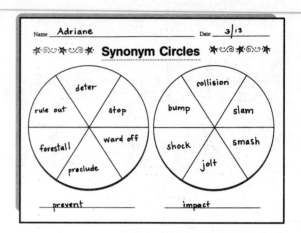

Name Adriane   Date 3/13
✦ Synonym Circles ✦

deter
rule out   stop
forestall   ward off
preclude
____prevent____

collision
bump   slam
shock   smash
jolt
____impact____

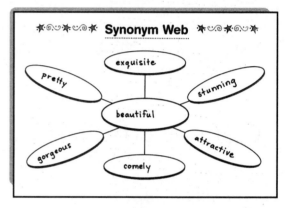

✦ Synonym Web ✦

exquisite
pretty   stunning
beautiful
gorgeous   attractive
comely

Cloze Exercises

In this cloze activity, students find unique, fitting words to fill in the blanks in a piece of writing. They get practice in choosing the best word to convey a particular meaning. Because different words appeal to people, each student will probably choose different words. This is great!

What to Do
Explain that in a cloze activity words are left out of the text. Students will choose a word to write in each blank. Have students work in pairs, and provide each pair with a copy of the reproducible on page 43. Students fill in words that could logically complete the thought. We share ideas as a whole group, and then I show them the words the poet had chosen where the blanks were.

TEACHER TIP
You can do this with any writing. Other poems that work well are "I'd Never Eat a Beet" and "Herman Sherman Thurman" by Jack Prelutsky. I hand out copies of the poem with certain words blanked out. I've also used a paragraph from a favorite author.

The Leaves

The leaves had a wonderful frolic.
They danced to the wind's loud song.
They whirled, and they floated, and scampered.
They circled and flew along.

The moon saw the little leaves dancing.
Each looked like a small brown bird.
The man in the moon smiled and listened.
And this is the song he heard.

The North Wind is calling, is calling,
And we must whirl round and round,
And then, when our dancing is ended,
We'll make a warm quilt for the ground.

Cloze Guidelines

* Leave the first and last sentence complete.
* Delete words in a random pattern.
* Delete words that most students will be able to supply from context. (Deleted words near the end of the sentence provide the most context clues.)
* Delete the words that appear frequently.
* Delete words only when the students know the concept.

Word-Choice Categories

Students will read good literature and then categorize words they think are really good choices.

What to Do

Students can work alone, in pairs, or in small groups. You can preselect chapters from literature for this activity or allow students to choose a book that you will approve. A class novel or book read at DEAR time can be ideal. Provide each student with a copy of

---

Name _____ Date _____

A Cloze Activity

Fill in the blanks in this poem.

The Leaves

The leaves had a wonderful frolic.

They danced to the wind's _____ song.

They whirled, and they _____ , and scampered.

They circled and flew along.

The moon saw the little leaves _____ .

Each looked like a _____ brown bird.

The man in the moon _____ and listened.

And this is the song he heard.

The North Wind is calling, is calling,

And we must _____ round and round,

And then, when our _____ is ended,

We'll make a warm quilt for the ground.

Teaching Elaboration and Word Choice: Scholastic Professional Books, page 43

Name _Janique_ Date _4/23_

Word-Choice Categories

While reading the chapters _1-3_ from the book _Missing May_

please find the most descriptive words that the author used to get his or her point across. Put these descriptive words in the most appropriate categories below. You may have to look them up before you categorize them.

CATEGORY	WORDS
Setting	"rusty old trailer on the face of a mountain"
Characters	May "hoisted herself out of "
Problems/Solution	
Other	
Humorous	fat bags of marshmallows
Serious	
Suspenseful	
Action Verbs	laboring, grunting, snipping
Adjectives/Adverbs	yellow-flowered, soft pink, glistening
Figurative Language (similes, metaphors, personification, exaggeration)	"made him look more scarecrow than ever"

Teaching Elaboration and Word Choice: Scholastic Professional Books, page 44

the reproducible on page 44. As they read, students should note great examples of word choice and list these words in the appropriate category on the sheet. Have the students discuss their findings, talking about which words were especially powerful. Tell them to add some favorite words to the word-catch section of their writing notebooks.

A to Z Alliteration Book

Students will create alliterative sentences that include descriptive adjectives and adverbs and compile these into a book.

What to Do

Reinforce the concepts of adjectives and adverbs by reading an alliterative book such as *Animalia* by Graeme Base to the class. After reading each page, ask students to name the adjectives and then the adverbs. Next choose a topic that the class is currently studying. We were doing a unit on the Middle Ages so we chose that topic. Together, brainstorm for a word on the topic for each letter of alphabet. Remind students of the concept of alliteration and ask them individually to come up with a sentence for each word that uses adjectives, adverbs, and alliteration. Have the students underline the adjectives and circle the adverbs. Finally, have them add pictures for some or all of their sentences and compile these into books. Here are two of the sentences my students wrote for our Middles Ages topic:

    A: Anxious Arthur argued atrociously.

    B: Bulky Beowulf barged boisterously over the broad bridge.

Sallying squires were swinging silvery swords.

The treasured tapestry told of timeless tales.

A Word a Day

With this activity, students learn at least one new word a day that they must use in a variety of ways that day. This activity enables students to remember that word and more easily store it in long-term memory.

What to Do

Not only do I teach words from literature and content areas, each morning I also teach a unique word of the day. I use the book *Vocabulary Cartoons* by Sam, Max, and Bryan Burchers. I copy and enlarge each page onto a transparency (the transparencies are also available for purchase), which is displayed when students first enter the classroom. Students then complete the Word a Day graphic organizer on page 45.

Discuss the word together and share students' sentence creations. Then encourage students to use that word during the day while talking to others. I give students a reward when they make a special effort to use the word in a discussion. Students may use a thesaurus to figure out synonyms and antonyms.

Poetry Perks

Writing poetry becomes an opportunity for students to make thoughtful word choices.

TOXIC
(TAHK sik)
having the effect of a poison

Sounds like: **SICK**

"Some snakebites are TOXIC and can make you SICK."

- ☐ Tobacco smoke is **TOXIC** to anyone who breathes it.
- ☐ A garbage dump contains many **TOXIC** materials such as oils and pesticide residues.
- ☐ Some shellfish like oysters contain a **TOXIN** that can make you sick if you eat them.

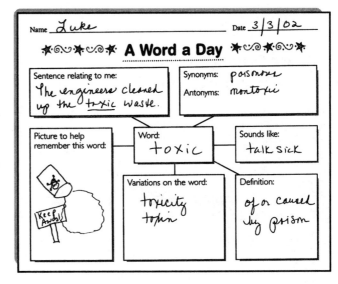

What to Do

Students reinforce what they've learned about a specific type of—or technique in—poetry, such as rhyming, haiku, limerick, sonnet, or diamante. After you've discussed types of poetry, have each student choose a poem they like that uses a particular format. Discuss and define the type as a class, identifying words that illustrate the type.

Type of Poem or Poetic Technique	Onomatopoeia
Definition	Words sound like their meaning.
Example	The Bells Hear the sledges with their bells— Silver bells! What a world of merriment their melody foretells! How they tinkle, tinkle, tinkle In the icy air of night! While the stars that oversprinkle All heavens, seem to twinkle... To the tintinnabulation that so musically wells, From the jingling and the tinkling of the bells. *By Edgar Allan Poe*

Type of Poem or Poetic Technique	Couplet
Definition	A simple rhymed two-line verse.
Example	Mourning doves are calling Springtime rains are falling

Type of Poem or Poetic Technique	Haiku
Definition	A three-line poem of 17 syllables (usually about nature).

Example	All leaves have fallen
	   (5 syllables)
	The tall old oak stands bravely
	   (7 syllables)
	Steeled to winter's cold
	   (5 syllables)

Type of Poem or Poetic Technique	Narrative
Definition	Poem that tells a story. Every other line rhymes.
Example	**Captain Kidd** This person in the gaudy clothes Is worthy Captain Kidd They say he never buried gold I think, perhaps, he did. They say it's all a story that His favorite little song, Was "Make these lubbers walk the plank!" I think, perhaps they're wrong. They say he never pirated Beneath the Skull-and-Bones. He merely traveled for this health And spoke in soothing tones. In fact, you'll read in nearly all The newer history books That he was mild as cottage cheese —But I don't like his looks. *By Rosemary and Stephen Vincent Benét*

Type of Poem or Poetic Technique	Cinquain
Definition	A 5-line poem with only 11 words.

Example	Friend
	   (1-word title)
	Caring helper
	   (2 words describing title)
	Always warmly smiling
	   (3 words describing action)
	Loving tower of support
	   (4 words describing a feeling)
	Comrade
	   (1-word synonym for title)

Type of Poem or Poetic Technique	Alliteration
Definition	An identical initial consonant sound is repeated throughout poem.
Example	**The Flea and the Fly** A flea and a fly got caught in a flue. Said the fly, "Let us flee." Said the flea, "Let us fly." So together they flew through a flaw in the flue

Type of Poem or Poetic Technique	Limerick
Definition	A five-line poem. The first, second, and fifth lines rhyme and have three beats. The third and fourth lines rhyme and have two beats. They are silly and humorous
Example	**Old Man With a Beard** There was an Old Man with a beard, Who said, "It is just as I feared!- Two Owls and a Hen, Four Larks and a Wren, Have all built their nests in my beard!" —*Edward Lear*

Choose a type of poetry and a particular subject that everyone will write about (winter, storms, school, and so on). Give each student a copy of the For the Poetry Book reproducible (page 46). We brainstorm for words related to the topic to use in students' poems. After they write a rough draft, they solicit and receive feedback. Remind students to use their word-catch words from their writing notebooks. When all the rough drafts are completed, students write their final copies and copy these into a class poetry book. We created a pop-up book, but you can use your own format.

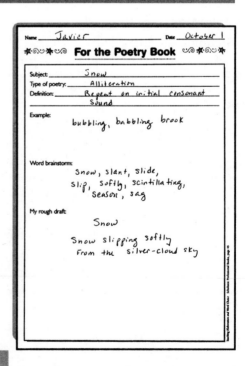

Name: Javier   Date: October 1
✦☾◉✷☾◉ **For the Poetry Book** ☾◉✷☾◉

Subject: Snow
Type of poetry: Alliteration
Definition: Repeat an initial consonant sound
Example: bubbling, babbling brook

Word brainstorm:
Snow, slant, slide, slip, softly, scintillating, season, sag

My rough draft:
Snow
Snow slipping softly
From the silver-cloud sky

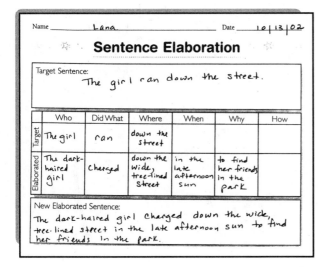

Elaborating Sentences

Students use a graphic organizer, based on an idea from Mary Howard's book *Writing With Children*, in order to evaluate words in a sentence they write.

What to Do

Have students write a simple target sentence on the Sentence Elaboration reproducible (page 47). By filling in the details, students will be able to create a new, more interesting sentence. This kind of evaluation will help the students choose better words for a particular sentence and naturally elaborate on their writing. You can pull out one of these sheets any time you see a sentence in a student's writing that needs more detail.

Name _____ Date _____

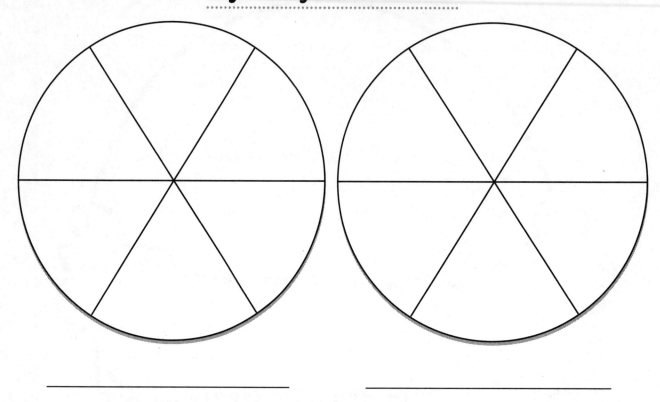

_____   _____

- -

★ ⊙ ‿ ★ ⊙ ‿ ★ **Synonym Web** ★ ‿ ⊙ ★ ⊙ ‿ ★

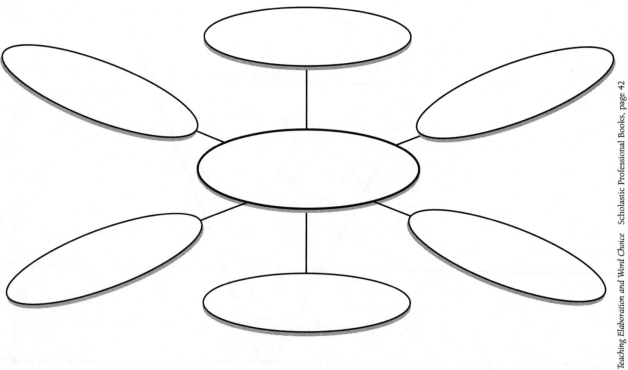

Name _____   Date _____

Fill in the blanks in this poem.

The Leaves

The leaves had a wonderful frolic.

They danced to the wind's _____ song.

They whirled, and they _____ , and scampered.

They circled and flew along.

The moon saw the little leaves _____.

Each looked like a _____ brown bird.

The man in the moon _____ and listened.

And this is the song he heard.

The North Wind is calling, is calling,

And we must _____ round and round,

And then, when our _____ is ended,

We'll make a warm quilt for the ground.

Name _____ Date _____

✴·Ꮽ·✴ **Word-Choice Categories** ✴·Ꮽ·✴

While reading the chapters _____ from the book _____

_____ ,

please find the most descriptive words that the author used to get his or her point across. Put these descriptive words in the most appropriate categories below. You may have to look them up before you categorize them.

CATEGORY	WORDS
Setting	
Characters	
Problems/Solution	
Other	
Humorous	
Serious	
Suspenseful	
Action Verbs	
Adjectives/Adverbs	
Figurative Language (similes, metaphors, personification, exaggeration)	

Name _____   Date _____

✦·◠◡◠·✦ A Word a Day ✦·◠◡◠·✦

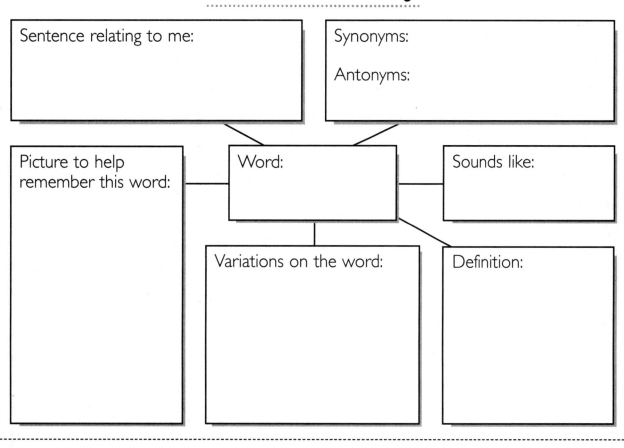

Sentence relating to me:

Synonyms:

Antonyms:

Picture to help remember this word:

Word:

Sounds like:

Variations on the word:

Definition:

Sentence relating to me:

Synonyms:

Antonyms:

Picture to help remember this word:

Word:

Sounds like:

Variations on the word:

Definition:

Name _____ Date _____

★ ✦ ✧ **For the Poetry Book** ✧ ✦ ★

Subject: _____

Type of poetry: _____

Definition: _____

_____

Example:

Word brainstorm:

My rough draft:

★·☯·✦·☯·✿ Sentence Elaboration ☯·✦·☯·✿

Target Sentence:

	Who	Did What	Where	When	Why	How
Target						
Elaborated						

New Elaborated Sentence:

Target Sentence:

	Who	Did What	Where	When	Why	How
Target						
Elaborated						

New Elaborated Sentence:

Chapter 4

Evaluation

We frequently hear that it's important to begin with the end in mind. In other words, you should have a plan or a goal before you start something. This couldn't be more true for writing. Writers want to know: What exactly am I trying to accomplish in this piece of writing? What are my strategies for accomplishing this plan or goal? How will my teacher or peers evaluate me on this writing?

To help students fully develop their word-choice and elaboration skills, they need the opportunity to set goals and the time to self-reflect. Most important, they need proper feedback from peers and from teachers—and from rubrics.

Finding the *Value* in Content

It's important to note that the word *value* is the base word in *evaluation*. Evaluation is the act of finding value in a piece of writing. A dull paper—even with perfect mechanics—is a paper with little value. Although conventions of writing are important, much time should be spent on creating interesting content. Students have to be excited about their topic if they're going to make their writing valuable. When evaluating, the editor starts asking questions about the content and begins to get to know the author and his or her interests. The main role of the teacher—listener, evaluator, or editor—is to find value within a student's writing and to share the findings with the author through feedback. There are many ways for students to seek and provide feedback.

The ones listed below are based on an article by Jane Hansen titled "Evaluation: The Center of Writing Instruction" that appeared in *The Reading Teacher*.

* Conference: Meet with a teacher, peer, or parent to answer questions about clarity (See Writing Conference Goals sheet on page 63.)
* Read Aloud: Have them read their writing aloud, with as much expression as possible, and give the audience time to respond with questions or I like statements.
* Reflect: Fill out a personal reflection sheet on their own writing. (These will vary according to the type of writing).

Promoting Writing Growth

It's important to use our evaluations—and students' self-evaluations—of their work to help students grow as writers. By studying students' writing, we learn which skills we should be teaching. By talking with them about their writing after they evaluate themselves, we can provide the help they need and want.

Here are several student-centered ways to promote writing growth:

* **Set Goals:** In a teacher-student conference, help the child generate possible goals and choose one to work on in a piece of writing. This gives the student the opportunity to prioritize and focus. For example, the student decides, "I will use more colorful adjectives before most nouns."

* **Ask Questions:** Have students reflect and evaluate themselves through a series of questions or rubric items that are relevant to the writing. You may want to have students help you write the rubrics. For example, when my students were writing a friendly letter describing their vacations, they set their own goals and asked themselves the following questions in their rubric:

—Did I include the five parts of a friendly letter: heading (writer's address and date), salutation, body, closing, and signature?

—Did I include an introduction and conclusion in the body of the letter?

—Do all my paragraphs include a main idea and supporting sentences?

—Did I describe a main event so that the reader can picture it in his or her mind?

—Did I use the five senses to create a description of the setting?

—Did I describe the people I've mentioned?

—Did I create dialogue with at least two sets of conversation?

—Did I use lively verbs and colorful adjectives?

—Did I include some onomatopoeic words?

—Are my spelling, grammar, and punctuation correct?

Your students' rubrics will reflect the type of writing they're doing and the skills they're developing.

* **Get Peer Feedback:** Allow students to give each other feedback through editing sheets, rubrics, and questions. For example, students can write down three things they liked about a classmate's paper and then suggest two growth opportunities. Students get excited about receiving this kind of feedback from a peer.

Rethinking the Role of the Teacher

All the recent education research has dramatically changed the roles of a teacher. Instead of just handing students their goals and writing assignments, we now know the importance of allowing students to choose their own goals and topics, and of providing students with the time for self-evaluation.

You can help students become independent thinkers and writers by showing them that you're a learner yourself. Share your own writing examples (and the goals you set for each piece) and solicit evaluation from your students. Thank students for taking the time to give thorough and thoughtful comments. This is a great way to model ways of giving helpful feedback without hurting the author's feelings.

✪ Examples of Evaluations

Now you know the goals of evaluations. I've included several ready-to-use models—including checklists and rubrics—you can use. You'll want to adjust them according to your students' needs and abilities. You can also create your own rubrics. I've done them myself, with the whole class and with individual students. Students can use the rubrics for self-evaluations or for editing their peers' work. You can use them to evaluate students for their grades.

Several of the rubrics and checklists I include at the end of this chapter are particularly helpful during Writing Process Step 5: Rereading for Sense and Readability. Students are reading their writing aloud to find missing words, too many words, or a boring, irrelevant word. They are also making sure they have included the requirements of the writing for a particular genre or format. I tell them ahead of time how they'll be evaluated and give them a copy of the rubric so they know the exact criteria I'll use.

Here are short descriptions of five evaluation tools.

SCAMPER Editing Sheet (page 53)
One way to enhance a student's creative thinking is by using the SCAMPER Editing Sheet. It was developed by Bob Eberle, a well-known author of activity books for gifted children. SCAMPER is an acronym for a series of thinking processes. Basically, you start with a particular object or idea and then think about ways to change it. I found a neat way to make it a self-reflection piece for

> **TEACHER TIP**
>
> To use SCAMPER for self-reflection, some kids need the acronym words left out because it is too much information. So sometimes I white out the acronym and just include the revision marks.

writing. Before students use this evaluation on their own, they need to practice
it several times as a class. Here's how.

Step 1. Teach each revision mark
separately. Find examples in writing
and show them on the overhead. Make
the appropriate marks where needed. For
example, you might have the following
sentence and box the cliche "cool, man":
"That was cool, man," said Jack. Explain
to the students that the box means to
substitute something better. Or for the
sentence "He was so ~~funny~~," you might
cross out (or X out) the word *funny* and
show students that means to replace it
with more figurative language: He was
as funny as a silly clown.

Step 2. When your students understand
all the SCAMPER marks, they can
begin using them to evaluate another
student's writing.

Word-Choice Checklist (page 54)

This sheet includes word choice, but
much more! If used for self-evaluation,
the students have to write which words
from their story were the best. This
forces them to evaluate each word
before they write it on the sheet. Also,
it encourages students to use their
word-catch resource more often. I tell
students that I'll look at this self-
evaluation checklist during their
writing conference.

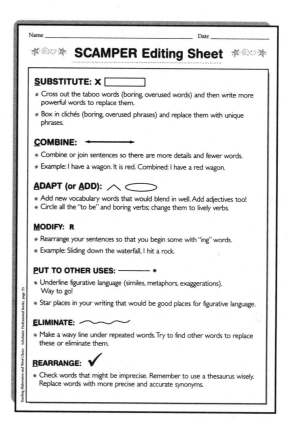

Rate Your Writing (page 55)

This student-directed rubric also asks students to rate their writing on a scale from 1 (Dull) to 5 (Great). Detailed characteristics of poor, moderate, and excellent writing are listed. Students can check the appropriate box when they finish their first draft and then set a goal for the final version. This rubric allows the writer to see clearly what his or her strengths and weaknesses are in a piece.

Rate Their Wording (page 56)

This rubric is for you to use to evaluate your students' word choice.

A Complete Writing Checklist
(pages 57–58)

This elaborate rubric is for the teacher to use. Students can use it after you've trained them in how to evaluate their writing for each of the areas listed. These are all the skills I expect students to practice in their writing.

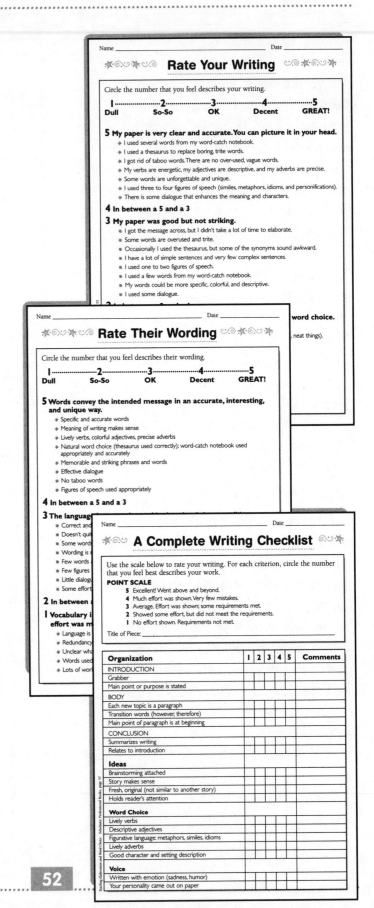

Name _____ Date _____

Rate Your Writing

Circle the number that you feel describes your writing.

1 .... 2 .... 3 .... 4 5
Dull   So-So   OK   Decent   GREAT!

5 My paper is very clear and accurate. You can picture it in your head.
- I used several words from my word-catch notebook.
- I used a thesaurus to replace boring, trite words.
- I got rid of taboo words. There are no over-used, vague words.
- My verbs are energetic, my adjectives are descriptive, and my adverbs are precise.
- Some words are unforgettable and unique.
- I used three to four figures of speech (similes, metaphors, idioms, and personifications).
- There is some dialogue that enhances the meaning and characters.

4 In between a 5 and a 3

3 My paper was good but not striking.
- I got the message across, but I didn't take a lot of time to elaborate.
- Some words are overused and trite.
- Occasionally I used the thesaurus, but some of the synonyms sound awkward.
- I have a lot of simple sentences and very few complex sentences.
- I used one to two figures of speech.
- I used a few words from my word-catch notebook.
- My words could be more specific, colorful, and descriptive.
- I used some dialogue.

Name _____ Date _____

Rate Their Wording

Circle the number that you feel describes their wording.

1 .... 2 .... 3 .... 4 5
Dull   So-So   OK   Decent   GREAT!

5 Words convey the intended message in an accurate, interesting, and unique way.
- Specific and accurate words
- Meaning of writing makes sense
- Lively verbs, colorful adjectives, precise adverbs
- Natural word choice (thesaurus used correctly); word-catch notebook used appropriately and accurately
- Memorable and striking phrases and words
- Effective dialogue
- No taboo words
- Figures of speech used appropriately

4 In between a 5 and a 3

3 The language
- Correct an...
- Doesn't qu...
- Some word...
- Wording is...
- Few words...
- Few figures...
- Little dialogu...
- Some effort...

2 In between...

1 Vocabulary i...
effort was m...
- Language is...
- Redundancy...
- Unclear wha...
- Words used...
- Lots of wor...

Name _____ Date _____

A Complete Writing Checklist

Use the scale below to rate your writing. For each criterion, circle the number that you feel best describes your work.
POINT SCALE
- **5** Excellent! Went above and beyond.
- **4** Much effort was shown. Very few mistakes.
- **3** Average. Effort was shown; some requirements met.
- **2** Showed some effort, but did not meet the requirements.
- **1** No effort shown. Requirements not met.

Title of Piece: _____

Organization	1	2	3	4	5	Comments
INTRODUCTION						
Grabber						
Main point or purpose is stated						
BODY						
Each new topic is a paragraph						
Transition words (however, therefore)						
Main point of paragraph is at beginning						
CONCLUSION						
Summarizes writing						
Relates to introduction						
Ideas						
Brainstorming attached						
Story makes sense						
Fresh, original (not similar to another story)						
Holds reader's attention						
Word Choice						
Lively verbs						
Descriptive adjectives						
Figurative language: metaphors, similes, idioms						
Lively adverbs						
Good character and setting description						
Voice						
Written with emotion (sadness, humor)						
Your personality came out on paper						

Name _____   Date _____

 # SCAMPER Editing Sheet

SUBSTITUTE: X ☐

* Cross out the taboo words (boring, overused words) and then write more powerful words to replace them.

* Box in clichés (boring, overused phrases) and replace them with unique phrases.

COMBINE: ←——————→

* Combine or join sentences so there are more details and fewer words.

* Example: I have a wagon. It is red. Combined: I have a red wagon.

ADAPT (or ADD): ⋀ ◯

* Add new vocabulary words that would blend in well. Add adjectives too!

* Circle all the "to be" and boring verbs; change them to lively verbs.

MODIFY: R

* Rearrange your sentences so that you begin some with "ing" words.

* Example: Sliding down the waterfall, I hit a rock.

PUT TO OTHER USES: ——————— *

* Underline figurative language (similes, metaphors, exaggerations). Way to go!

* Star places in your writing that would be good places for figurative language.

ELIMINATE: 〜〜〜〜〜

* Make a wavy line under repeated words. Try to find other words to replace these or eliminate them.

REARRANGE:

* Check words that might be imprecise. Remember to use a thesaurus wisely. Replace words with more precise and accurate synonyms.

Name _____ Date _____

✴ ❂ ✴ **Word-Choice Checklist** ✴ ❂ ✴

✴ I used the following lively, unique verbs: _____

_____

✴ I used the following adjectives to describe nouns more accurately:

Setting adjectives: _____

Character adjectives: _____

Other adjectives: _____

✴ I don't have any taboo words. Instead, I used: _____

_____

✴ These are words that I put great thought into: _____

_____

✴ I used the following similes and metaphors: _____

_____

✴ My favorite words in this writing are: _____

_____

✴ I used the following unique phrases: _____

_____

_____

✴ I can mentally picture the following part of my story: _____

_____

_____

✴ My favorite dialogue sentences are: _____

_____

✴ I feel that I achieved my writing goal by doing the following: _____

_____

✴ After careful examination, I am going to change the following words

(I will use a thesaurus to find some neat synonyms): _____

_____

Name _____   Date _____

 # Rate Your Writing

Circle the number that you feel describes your writing.

1···············**2**···············**3**···············**4**···············**5**
Dull   **So-So**   **OK**   **Decent**   **GREAT!**

5 My paper is very clear and accurate. You can picture it in your head.
* ✳ I used several words from my word-catch notebook.
* ✳ I used a thesaurus to replace boring, trite words.
* ✳ I got rid of taboo words. There are no overused, vague words.
* ✳ My verbs are energetic, my adjectives are descriptive, and my adverbs are precise.
* ✳ Some words are unforgettable and unique.
* ✳ I used three to four figures of speech (similes, metaphors, idioms, and personifications).
* ✳ There is some dialogue that enhances the meaning and characters.

4 In between a 5 and a 3

3 My paper was good but not striking.
* ✳ I got the message across, but I didn't take a lot of time to elaborate.
* ✳ Some words are overused and trite.
* ✳ Occasionally I used the thesaurus, but some of the synonyms sound awkward.
* ✳ I have a lot of simple sentences and very few complex sentences.
* ✳ I used one to two figures of speech.
* ✳ I used a few words from my word-catch notebook.
* ✳ My words could be more specific, colorful, and descriptive.
* ✳ I used some dialogue.

2 In between a 3 and a 1

1 My paper is confusing, with no effort to improve my word choice.
* ✳ The reader is wondering, What did the author mean by this?
* ✳ My words and phrases are vague (For example: We did a lot of fun, neat things).
* ✳ All of my sentences are simple and include few details.
* ✳ I did not use my word-catch notebook or a thesaurus.
* ✳ My writing makes it hard to picture exactly what is happening.
* ✳ I overused several words and used taboo words.
* ✳ My story doesn't hold the audience's attention very well.
* ✳ I didn't include any dialogue.
* ✳ I didn't include any figures of speech.

Name _____ Date _____

Rate Their Wording

Circle the number that you feel describes their wording.

1 .... **2** .... **3** .... **4** **5**
Dull   **So-So**   **OK**   **Decent**   **GREAT!**

5 Words convey the intended message in an accurate, interesting, and unique way.

* Specific and accurate words
* Meaning of writing makes sense
* Lively verbs, colorful adjectives, precise adverbs
* Natural word choice (thesaurus used correctly); word-catch notebook used appropriately and accurately
* Memorable and striking phrases and words
* Effective dialogue
* No taboo words
* Figures of speech used appropriately

4 In between a 5 and a 3

3 The language has meaning and is clear, but it is not striking.

* Correct and adequate words
* Doesn't quite hold audience's attention
* Some words are descriptive, colorful, and lively
* Wording is not very natural (awkward)
* Few words are from the word-catch notebook
* Few figures of speech (or used inaccurately)
* Little dialogue that enhances the writing
* Some effort made to use better word choice

2 In between a 3 and a 1

1 Vocabulary is limited, meaning of writing is unclear, and little effort was made to improve word choice.

* Language is vague (taboo words used, simple sentences, little or no elaboration)
* Redundancy (words used over and over)
* Unclear what the author is really trying to say
* Words used incorrectly
* Lots of work needs to be done in order to improve the word choice

Name _____ Date _____

 # A Complete Writing Checklist

Use the scale below to rate your writing. For each criterion, circle the number that you feel best describes your work.

POINT SCALE

5 Excellent! Went above and beyond.

4 Much effort was shown. Very few mistakes.

3 Average. Effort was shown; some requirements met.

2 Showed some effort, but did not meet the requirements.

1 No effort shown. Requirements not met.

Title of Piece: _____

Organization	1	2	3	4	5	Comments
INTRODUCTION						
Grabber						
Main point or purpose is stated						
BODY						
Each new topic is a paragraph						
Transition words (however, therefore)						
Main point of paragraph is at beginning						
CONCLUSION						
Summarizes writing						
Relates to introduction						
Ideas						
Brainstorming attached						
Story makes sense						
Fresh, original (not similar to another story)						
Holds reader's attention						
Word Choice						
Lively verbs						
Descriptive adjectives						
Figurative language: metaphors, similes, idioms						
Lively adverbs						
Good character and setting description						
Voice						
Written with emotion (sadness, humor)						
Your personality came out on paper						

A Complete Writing Checklist (cont.)

Organization	1	2	3	4	5	Comments
No sentence fragments						
Dialogue is natuaral, labeled correctly						
Sentences vary in length—complex						
No run-on sentences						
Form						
Name on paper						
Title centered on top line and in caps						
Margins on both sides of paper						
Paragraphs indented						
Correctness						
Capitalization of beginning sentences; proper nouns						
Verb tense agreement (present, past, future)						
Subject/verb agreement: "He doesn't" not "He don't"						
Spelling						
Sentence punctuation						
Personal Goal						
My writing goal:						
Total Points						

Chapter 5

The Writing Notebook

I want to make sure that I'm emphasizing word choice in every piece of my students' writing, but I take care not to forget the other components of good writing. Because there are so many things to remember to craft a good piece of writing, I created a system for my students—writing notebooks—that organizes and includes all of the important elements of writing.

Each student brings to school a one-inch wide, three-ring binder. The student's name with the notebook title (for example, Nicole's Writing Notebook) goes on the front of the binder (many binders have a clear slide-in sheet attached that a name page can slip into). Also, write the student's full name on the side of their binder, so that when you store them upright, they're easy to find. We make our own tabs by cutting pieces of

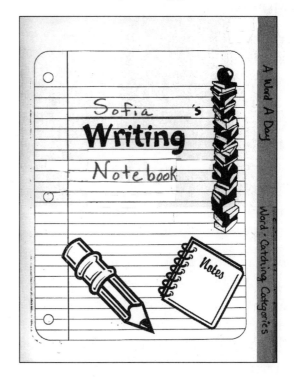

9" by 12" construction paper in half, two-hole punching these on one side, and then writing the subject of that section on the edge that extends beyond the regular 8½" by 11" notebook-size paper. Each tab section is a different color—red for Notetaking, for example—to make all our notebooks similar. I store the binders on a bookshelf, and every time we write, I assign three students to pass them out. I expect the writing notebooks to be on students' desks whenever they're writing.

Following is a brief description of the contents of each section in the writing notebook. You'll want to tailor your notebooks to fit the grade level and particular needs and interests of your students.

Section I: Organizational Sheets

1. A Word a Day. Have students keep copies of their completed Word a Day reproducibles (see page 45) in their notebooks. These are great for review.

2. Word-Catch Categories. A photocopy of the word-catch list (see page 20) as well as student-created lists (see page 19) follow the Word a Day reproducibles. You might want to have students put these lists first (clipped with a binder clip) in the front pocket of the notebook since you want students to refer to them often.

3. Writing Conference Goals. This sheet (page 63), which students fill out as we conference, goes into the binder. I copy (front to back) two sheets per student for the whole year.

4. Synonym Circles for Taboo Words. I provide students with six copies of these circles (see page 42). Of course more can be added at any time, and students can easily draw these circles themselves on notebook paper. When we come up with a vague, overused, or boring word that needs to be replaced, we complete a circle. It's a great way to remind students to think about word choice throughout the year.

5. Spelling Word Bank. I tell my students that a good writer tries to learn from his or her mistakes, and I hold them accountable for misspelled words in their writing. After a student's rough draft is edited, have him or her write all of the misspelled words in

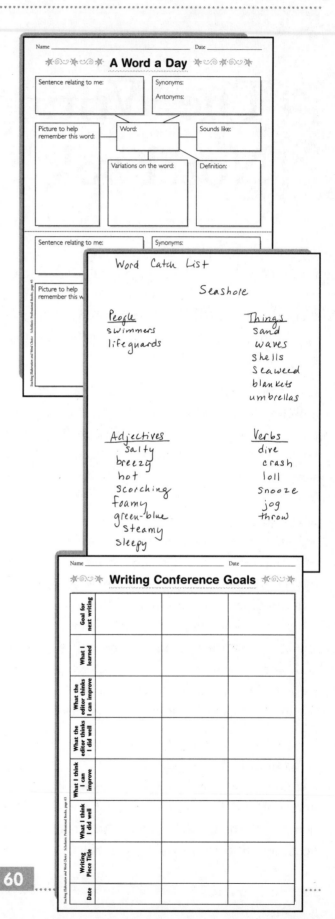

alphabetical order in this spelling word bank section. By doing this, students are likely to remember a word they had trouble with before and want to use again in their word bank. If they look up words there as they need them, they'll begin to grow as spellers. I frequently remind students to use this resource. I also give spelling tests on students' personal lists once a month.

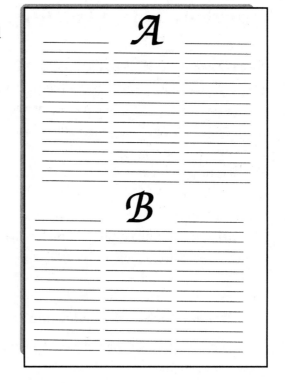

Section II: Note-Taking

1. Note-taking Paper. Students put lined paper in the front part of this section. As they do more and more writing and we have mini-lessons on various writing rules and procedures, they write notes here. These notes serve as a good reference and reinforcement when they get stuck while they're writing. Here are some possible note-taking topics:

* characteristics of good introductions
* characteristics of good conclusions
* parts of speech
* the nine-step writing process
* about sentences—capitalization, complete thoughts, punctuation, subject-verb agreement
* main idea and supporting ideas in a paragraph
* examples of complex sentences and sentence combinations
* punctuation rules

2. Reminder Pages. I also photocopy the following sheets for students to use as needed.

* List of writing topics
* Word-Choice Checklist (page 54)
* Computer shortcuts and reminders for when final copies are typed
* Proofreading marks (page 64)
* Confusing homonyms and homophones

Section III: My Writing

Story Pages. Students put several blank dividing tabs in this section (one per story). I find it easier to keep everything related to each story in its own section. For example, one of these tabs might be labeled "Mystery Story." In this tabbed section, the following items are three-hole punched and stored:

* Brainstorm sheets
* Student checklists
* Editor's remark sheet
* Rough draft
* Final copy (I make a photocopy for the notebook since I like to keep the originals in bound class books, in portfolios, or displayed on the walls in some creative way.)

Benefits of Writing Notebooks

The benefits of writing notebooks are numerous. Here are a few reasons I like to use them. They:

* Allow you to keep track of growth in all areas of writing quickly and easily.
* Provide a quick way to see if goals are being met by looking through writings and evaluations.
* Provide students with ways to find the answers to questions themselves.
* Encourage students to use the word-catch category resource because it's accessible in a prominent place in the notebook.
* Keep you and your students organized so the various stages of writing never get lost (a teacher's worst nightmare!).
* Are perfect to show student progress at parent conferences.

Most important, writing notebooks help students integrate the principles of good writing with the ability to choose dynamic, precise words in their writing—an aspect of teaching writing that is frequently overlooked.

Name _____ Date _____

✯✿✽ Writing Conference Goals ✯✿✽

Date	Writing Piece Title	What I think I did well	What I think I can improve	What the editor thinks I did well	What the editor thinks I can improve	What I learned	Goal for next writing

Proofreading Marks

Editor's Marks	Meaning	Example
≡	capitalize	they visited the Grand Canyon.
/	make it lowercase	Ellen was late for the Party.
Sp.	spelling mistake	January is the first (moth) of the year.
⊙	add a period	Manuel plays hockey ⊙
ℯ	delete (remove)	Nick is in the the seventh grade.
∧	add a word	The red car is missing a wheel.
⌃	add a comma	He ate a banana an apple, and a pear.
∽	reverse words or letters	A whale is a mammal sea.
⌃'	add an apostrophe	Angels father came to the game.
"∧ / "∧	add quotation marks	You're late, yelled the bus driver.
#	make a space	Alex plays the guitar.
⌢	close the space	The butter fly landed on the flower.
¶	begin a new paragraph	to see. ¶ Finally, I feel . . .